Time Management For Cats

ALISON F. BOWMAN

Alison Frances Bowman © 2013.
First edition: July 2013

A Self Help for Cats Book
selfhelpforcats.net
selfhelpforcats@gmail.com

First Published:
"Fang Shui," *San Francisco Chronicle,* November 25, 2005
"Fit or Cat?" published as "Here, Humongous Kitty, Kitty, Kitty"
     San Francisco Chronicle, May 20, 2006,

ISBN: 0615805531
ISBN-13: 978-0615805535
Ebook ISBN: 9781301491582 (@Smashwords.com)

For Herman, Brody, and Hank,
and all the other struggling cats out there.

We are obligated to help the animals
whenever they require it.

-St. Francis de Assisi

The heresy of one age becomes
the orthodoxy of the next.

-Helen Keller

Dogs have owners
Cats have staff.

--bumper sticker

CONTENTS

1

The Time Management for Cats Breakthrough: Why Now Is an Extremely Exciting Time to Be a Cat

What exactly is time to cats? Does the future exist for them? How can I put my cat to work?

Generations of humans have asked these questions. Finally we have some answers. That's why right now is an extremely exciting time to be a cat!

Up to now, cats have been an undeveloped resource lying fallow on couches across the country -- overweight, under-stimulated, and left to hunt house-flies, or as we call them at my place, "little birds." But the pendulum is starting to turn on our furry little friends...

Times are leaner, and meaner. Hard work is "in;" 24-hour naps are "out." Everyone needs an edge in this economy just to pull their own weight. If you've been slaving away while your cat sleeps away, I'm sure you'll agree: It's high time we bring back the fabled "Working Cat," and in a totally new, modern and technological context.

The long rest is over, kitties. It's time to wake up, really wake up, and make a world where cat-human syncro-creativity is unleashed, uncensored, and *on fire*! And why not wake up, kitties, and start enjoying the same phenomenal developments in self-improvement that human beings have been honing themselves to near-perfection with for years? There's no good reason people alone should benefit from the likes of Feng Shui, Extreme Makeovers, The South Shore Lake Lap Diet, etc., etc., etc.

Until now, cats have been largely left out of the self-help gains of recent decades. A few books try to raise kitty consciousness, sure, but I have to wonder about cats too *busy* to read poetry, too *disorganized* to learn French? The offerings have been spotty at best. A practical book like *Time Management for Cats* has been omitted from the selection—until now.

That's precisely why now is an extremely exciting time to be a cat! The *Time Management for Cats* program includes the latest proven cutting-edge techniques for getting more out of your cat's life starting today. And thanks to this incredible book, putting your cat to work has never been easier or more enjoyable.

If you've been looking for a home-based hobby for fun and profit, consider this: If you have a cat, you don't need stinky chickens or destructive goats. *Time Management for Cats* may not be exactly what you call "simple money," but it's far less backbreaking than, say, planting a farm on your hazard strip.

Of course, like any worthwhile endeavor, it's going to take some effort on everyone's part to reverse decades of contrarian "catitude." But with this book and some time and sweat and maybe a little bit of blood (yours), you will be well on your way! Well on your way, that is, to understanding that managing your cat's time is the #1 best way to spend *your* time.

Welcome to the future, felines.

2

The Inevitability of Cat Time Management: A History and Future for the Working Cat

Have you ever looked at your cat and wondered, what were you put here for, kitty? What are cats *supposed* to be doing here on Planet Earth?

All theories aside, let's focus on the facts: Cats weren't built to be permanently at leisure and they surely can't expect to keep sponging-off the human race forever and ever. Fortunately, no matter how unproductive cats may have been in recent decades, these sweet, crafty and talented creatures could be getting a lot more done around the house, and even the nation, the planet—and beyond! In fact, there is a historical imperative that they start to do so *immediately*. Allow me to show you exactly what I mean as we delve into a little house-cat history.

The Working Cat:
Toward a Historical Materialist Misunderstanding

As oxymoronic as it may sound, the term "Working Cat" is not something I invented. The cat we call "domestic" has enjoyed a long history of full employment. The non-working status of most modern house cats is merely a recent development, a historic cul-de-sac, a bad trend on its way out.

Nowadays cats can seem fairly divorced from their long, proud working history. Sometimes it seems cats' whole purpose in life is to hold down the bed covers. But lying dormant in your dormantly-lying cat is humanity's most cunning ally who has served us bravely for millennia, and with a lot of style.

From what archeologists gather, cats and people have found each other useful enough to tolerate for something in the neighborhood of 10,000 years. This monumental collaboration between people and pussycats predates the history tablets, so we can only imagine how that first intrepid cat wandered in from the wild to strike a bargain with an inscrutable, two-legged furless.

We used to blame Ancient Egypt's grain silos, redolent with rodents, for drawing out the first wild cat population from their forest-tree homes. But evidence now shows a Mediterranean island cat to be the first-known domesticator of man. Wherever that crucial first contact occurred, the earliest cat-human encounter may well have been a purely-economic arrangement, simple room-and-board for services rendered. Cats provided ecological pest management, quickly earning a valued place at man's compound, albeit in the barn at first.

Maybe there was no love lost in those early, primitive arrangements, but soon enough, love with a big "L" would be found. Wherever cats and humans mixed company there was destined to be chemistry, and the rest is history.

As nameless as the intrepid first barn cat is the experimental first human who took the first kitten into her house and heart, sparking the transformation from reclusive barn stalker to today's zen-generator of intelligent purring affection. What started out as strictly a rats-for-roof deal at some point became something far more than either cat or human bargained for.

Over these last 10 millennia or so, cats and people have come a long way together. But the *Time Management for Cats* program promises we ain't seen nothing yet, baby.

The American Cat:
A Legacy of Pride, Freedom, and Leisure

Flashing forward to the great social experiment known as the USA, we see that cats have come full circle, and have the fat, round bellies to prove it. What happened to our working cats in a country of working people? Although cats have never been more in tune with their human beings, and have laid the foundation for an abiding cat-human love, they have also suffered increasingly in recent years from being under-realized and subjected to people's low-to-non-existent expectations of them.

Even so, it is clear that American Cats, like their human counterparts, have developed and thrived in the New World. Now, it is far beyond the scope of this book to look at *all* of American Cat history, which in truth can get a bit fuzzy in places. However, there is one quintessentially American Cat whose history demonstrates the kind of independent spirit that being an American Cat is all about. I refer to the tenacious little tiger from New England, also known as the great Maine Coon. I happen to live with a Maine Coon cat, and as anyone who has ever known a Maine Coon cat knows: There is no escaping the heroic legacy of these gentle giants.

I knew nothing about Brody's breed, however, when I rescued him from his kitten misery at the San Francisco SPCA on Thanksgiving week more than a few years back. Yes, he was gorgeous and exotic, a long-haired tabby with an expressive bobcat face. But what drew me to him in a room of noisy kittens was his extreme unhappiness with his caged predicament. Brody's little body positively telegraphed gloom. When I asked to hold him, he squirmed away under the bank of the cages and could be retrieved only with some difficulty and a scolding for me from the attendant.

Clearly, Brody needed to breakout. I sensed that if I took this four-month-old freedom-fighter home, he would be a devoted friend forever and end up returning the favor a thousand fold. And since that first day when he finally emerged from under my dresser, sniffed around, and walked straight across the room to plant a kiss on my nose, well, what can I say? Brody is emotionally profound. He always knows exactly what to say and when I need him to just shut up and purr.

As deeply as this determined tabby weaseled his way into my heart, the Maine Coon cat's fascinating history would sink its fangs into my curiosity. Turns out, the roots of Brody Bowcat run real deep, possibly even all the way back to the forests of Viking Norway where his reclusive ancestors once behaved like squirrelly forest-monkeys. Yes, if you buy the Norwegian Forest Cat theory of Maine Coon origin, Brody is the real friggïn thing.

However, the manner in which Maine acquired its state cat is not at all clear, providing a contentious question among Maine Coon cat historians. In my favored theory, a renegade Norwegian Forest Cat or two hitchhiked on a Viking ship to the New World, eventually settling in the New England area. But a conflicting explanation of no minor intrigue claims that Maine's Coon cat came to America care of Marie Antoinette. The Queen, it's said, had her longhaired darlings sent to Canada as she readied to flee revolutionary France. Everyone knows how that ended. She got separated from her baggage, among other things.

The ship's captain, after learning of Marie's demise, is alleged to have set her cats loose in wild, wooly New England. Was he one of these Maine-mad mainiacs looking to create a Maine Coon cat legacy for the future state? Or did he merely seize the first opportunity to dump the Queen's litter, which otherwise may have arrived in Canada cat-a non-grata? Whatever the Captain's motivation, a new American cat race was born and the native small-critter populations would never have it the same.

Despite their possible barbarian or royalist beginnings, the Maine Coon cat took to America like a true Yank. These large, tough, walking fur-slabs could take civilization or leave it, and some became barn cats while others "went native." Maine Coon cats were in fact so scrappy, it was rumored that they were actually part raccoon. Physically impossible, yes, but adds to the mystery, no?

Americans initially embraced their very own original Maine Coon cats, who showed as much pioneering toughness as the settlers themselves. When the first American Cat Shows rolled around, Maine Coon cats swiped up all the prizes. But the nation's tastes soon turned against the "macho," backwoods farm cats from the North. Within a few years, these large, shedding examples of hearty New England stock would be pushed off the podium and out of cat shows entirely to make room for more delicate, prissier breeds.

Of course, the Maine Coon cat could give a rat's what's-it about the so-called decline of its public image, what with a whole nation to explore, grasslands to stalk, fat bird herds to decimate, not to mention the establishment of an entire industry devoted to the care and feeding of cats.

One day, the great, great, great, great (x10) grand-daddy of my cat Brody heard the train whistle calling and decided to head west. Or maybe he was a 49er cat who came during the Gold Rush, a Bangor dock kitty on a boat to California. After coming around the Cape on a diet of scurvacious ship vermin, he saw the great Golden Gate and decided to cash it in. However this New England snow cat found his way to Frisco, there is no doubt he felt the California sun on his matted fur, sniffed around and knew he'd arrived in the land of milk and wet food.

I can see him thinking to himself, "This is great. A cat can really benefit from all this rampant gold rushing." And in fact California has been a fertile utopia for the hearty, adventurous felines of all breeds who have found their way here. At first they feasted on the vermin attracted to all the disorganized humanity. Later, they ingratiated themselves into the burgeoning working classes. Soon enough, they were sleeping in our beds and hogging the covers. Just try putting that genie back in the bottle.

"The Free Ride is Over, Pussy"

The point of this little history lesson is that cats aren't nearly as listless and unambitious as they might act. For centuries, these little pilgrims have been sailing the high seas at our sides, spreading their influence to the planet's far reaches.

I mean, for goddess' sake, in ancient Egypt cats rose to the highest ranks of society and were worshipped as deities! And even practical peoples have recognized that cats have a really important job to do around town and farm. Medieval Europe had to learn the hard way that cats are a crucial part of human life. After massacring thousands of cats as witches, people suffered the black plague, spread by enlarged rat populations. One in four people died hideously-painful deaths, and the survivors were forced to admit there are worse things in life than feline bewitchment.

This important ally to humanity, however, is perishing in apartments around the globe. Yes, cats seem vocationally obsolete thanks to county vector departments, exterminators, etc. But that is no excuse for these intelligent creatures to mope about. It's time to end the housecat welfare system. Turn to your cat now and say, "Back to work, Pussy. The free ride is over!"

The *Time Management for Cats* Historic Imperative Outline

Pre 7500 BC—Reclusive Wild Cats Await History from Their Trees

Circa 7500 BC—Mediterranean Cat Woos Owner, Makes Headlines 9500 Years Later

Circa 2000 BC—Egyptian Grain Silos Attract Fat Rats & Itinerant Wild Cats

Circa 1000 AD—Vikings Cats Possibly Let Loose on the Future New England

Middle Ages—Medieval Witch Hunt Cat Massacres Lead to Hellish Plague Deaths

1790s—French Revolution: Marie Antoinette Separated From Cats, Baggage, etc.

1849—California Gold Rush, Start of Western Cat Migration aka Catifest Destiny

Post-WWII—Cat Agenda Obscured in Full-Time Leisure Experiment

1994—Author Rescues Deep-Thinker Maine Coon Cat Brody from SPCA

2013— *Time Management for Cats* published, Dormant Cat Agenda Revived

The Future: ?? Sky is limit...

3

The Gentle Art of Managing Your Cat's Time: Terms and Tools for Common Cat/Time Conundrums

Time. The Future. Work. Discipline. These may all be foreign concepts to your cat. But that's about to change...

We are almost ready to dive into The Program. Before we launch Tigger headlong into his new and improved lifestyle, however, let's let him bask in his last moments of blissful ignorance in order to review some of the concepts central to managing your cat's time to its utmost. In this section, I take a lot of big concepts and break them into small paragraphs.

TIME & CATS: *Time Management for Cats* is the result of a lot of time spent thinking about time and cats. Your author had to 'go to the mountain' to hone the plan that will get your cats on the fast track to success. And while I was there, I asked myself the hard questions, like: "Is time better tamed with a whisper, like a horse, or drummed and dazzled into submission, like a dragon?" And, "Can one crack a whip at time and still stop to savor life's flower fragrances?"

One of the most important things to remember as you set out is this: It is entirely possible that time moves at a very different rate for cats than it does for people. For all we know, a cat's day could last as long as a week or may zip by in a few short nanoseconds. As a result, we must never assume *anything* about cats and time. Something to keep it in mind moving forward.

TIME MANAGEMENT: Here's a slippery concept that used to be so simple. It used to be easy to assume time could be managed. But now after decades of blindly buying time-management best-sellers by the freight load, the public consciousness has stirred from our planning-induced stupor to ask: Is time even really *manageable*??

Well, I say whoever came up with that question sure must have had some spare time on their hands. This whole line of thought is clearly a result of the very gains made in the art and science of time management.

Practically a glut of it.

Still, I will admit that in my more indulgent moments, even I can ponder such far-out questions as whether anyone can really manage time or whether time, heaven forbid, manages us?

Ultimately, as usual with these matters, after thinking long and hard I decided on this approach: "Let's not get too philosophical. Let's assume time can be managed, what the heck? The alternatives simply suck too much."

Assuming we can manage time then, it follows that we can manage our cats' time, too. Believe it or not, your cat also wants to find better ways to spend its time. Until the day he succumbs to a life of abject boredom, a cat is always looking for ways to use time to expand its mind and grow. Ask yourself, have you been helping or hindering your cat's desire to make the best use of his time? To this point, when was the last time you brought your cat to the public library?

SCHEDULING: Here is another thing to remember as you start any *Time Management for Cats* plan: Your cat already has a schedule, even if no one recognizes it as such. Your cat may appear to be letting the world pass him by on a daily basis, but in truth he is far more attuned to the passing of day and night than you and I.

If you bother to notice, you'll probably find that your

cat's "on" hours will display a sure nocturnal streak. Centuries of evolution have prepared your cat for the graveyard shift. Think twice before attempting to turn the tide and find him a day job.

THE FUTURE: The future is something your cat may not have thought about before. But your cat may *have* no future if he keeps it up.

That's why you need to keep reading—and stop worrying! There is always a place in the future for a cat who can stay up to date with their technical skills and learn to evolve. Simply follow the easy *Time Management for Cats* steps outlined in this book, and you're set.

WORK: "Cats and work" may sound at first like "oil and water" to the untrained ear. But cats and work need not be mortal, repelling, enemy forces. Innovation is, after all, this country's middle name.

The fact is, cats *need* work every little bit as much as we *need them to* work. You see, the cat's singular mousing skills have not merely lost their value to people; they have in fact become a liability. All that predatory energy needs to be turned into positive action or it will be turned toward the small wild-animal population or that other cat obsession, the food bowl, and its promise of a premature death of the personality.

Why should such a charming creature suffer such a tragically-dull fate? Just what is blocking this charismatic, independent, loyal personality from going far in this world?

When I think of the services my cats provide and their value to me, and what each one means to me, and how little they ask in return—well, I start to feel that I don't even *have* to put my cats to work. But this type of work they do, this emotional labor, traditionally counts for nothing or everything, but it never counts for something—it won't fill the kibble-hole. See: DEBT.

DEBT: Another difficult concept for cats to grasp. We can blame this on lack of experience. Cats, like other animals, live exclusively on a paw-to-mouth basis—the cash-only arrangement of the natural world. Leave it to humans to come up with credit and credit-card living. (I am not recommending that you get your cat a credit card.)

CATS & THE "NO" CONCEPT: Experts agree that learning how and when to say "no" is a key tenet of any time management plan. Apparently, you can "yes" your way out of having any time left to manage. Although this may not be a problem for your cat *yet*, you should still get started enlightening him on the many benefits of knowing how to say "no."

Right now, your cat probably already has effective ways of expressing the negative, however lacking in tact and subtlety these methods may be. Cats can tend to overstate their case, resorting to use of "the hiss," "the yowl," and "the swipe," when all they really are trying to tell you is, "Nein," "Nix It," or "That's a negatory, Big Ben." If only they could learn to say "no," it would avoid so much of the … bleeding.

Clearly cats have no natural propensity against saying "no." "No" is part of every cat's vocabulary, even if they have no word for it. Studies indicate that cats who could say "no," would say "no."

If anyone who thinks cats need to learn how to say "no" says that cats don't know the word "no," then they are lying. Cats know "no." They just don't know how to say "no," that is, to speak the word "no," because they certainly do say it all the time, and I have the scars to prove it.

People need to learn to take "no" for an answer from their cats, and yes, I include myself in the "people" category here. When it comes to cats, "no" most certainly does not mean "yes." "Yes" is a whole other bag of worms, and, yes, cats need to learn how to say "yes," as well as "no," but the situation is not nearly as imperative, for obvious reasons.

Cats know when *you* say "no," or are about to say "no." They just know. It's not a psychic thing. They know when "no" is called for, usually because they are all-too aware that they are misbehaving.

If you want to keep a cat on his toes, there is a thing called "Kitty No!" which consists of water in a spray bottle. It can work on a hard case as long as he remains ignorant of its source. However, if kitty catches on that the "Kitty No!" comes from you, it's the cat-discipline equivalent of shaving Samson.

Cats & Discipline: Don't Try This at Home

Now let me turn to another tricky topic, and an important one: the dilemma of disciplining your cat. I have heard about some thorny feline problems in my day. Trust me, people, tick-off the cat and you'll be sorry. The cat is remarkably well equipped for expressing negative feelings in a message you will not misinterpret or easily forget, particularly if it involves his poop and your pillow.

A cat owner can avoid such problems by having a respectful relationship with the cat. In other words, letting the cat do almost anything it damn well wants to do. This method has worked just fine for me, and I don't have any nasty tit-for-tats with my cats. The secret is, I almost never discipline them, and they are *extremely* well trained.

An example of this is the only hard cat rule I have: "No

kitties on the kitchen counters." My little angels know this rule so well, they only ever visit the prohibited zone when they believe I am either asleep or out.

Unfortunately, we live in an epoch of exceedingly-controlled personal environments. The untold victims of the epidemic quest to turn the home into a temple of comfort and class are the loved ones—the incalculable millions of normal-level-messy people who suffer in the shadows of the picture-perfect home. Cat is not immune to this tyranny of over order. On the contrary, kitty is often subject to the worst kind of boring, arbitrary rules like "stay off the bed," "don't shred the couch," and "don't drink from the toilet."

A few ground rules are okay (and the toilet drinking really *can't be* good), but anyone who is disciplining a cat every day is placing a big, mean order for trouble at the cat attitude to-go window. Here's some advice before you start and lose World War Pee: Let your cat live in your house. To your cat, your domain is their entire existence, where to you it is only the place you land your sorry self at the end of the day. You may think that everything needs to be in order there, that it's the only place where you have any control in this crazy, messed-up world. But come on, stop kidding yourself. You don't have any control there either!

That is what a cat is for. The cat is proof that chaos lives and works to mess you up. Sometimes the chaos walks in on four adorable paws, stands on the kitchen table, and showers vomit onto your perfect, just-polished floor. But the chaos, even here, is made of purr, that's pure, love. Now come on, isn't this shedding slice of stardust, this endearing personality of the blue planet, worth a million perfect living rooms and clean kitchen floors?

You don't have to be a psychic to know what your cat wants. He wants to be adored and given free reign of *his* kingdom. You are a fool not to give it to him.

Here is a rhyme to help you remember this lesson:

Cats & Discipline
Rhymes with
Nitroglycerin

Hand is Key for Greater Cat Productivity

So the stick won't work, and cats are immune to carrots. Even so, chances are good you have a whole set of tools on you that were made to work wonders on your cat.

If your cat could talk he would tell you, "Never underestimate the power and value of the human hand." People get so wrapped up yapping about how great the human brain is, we tend to overlook the things right under (and occasionally in) our noses: The old high-fivers.

Where would we be without our obedient meat puppets at the end of these long, bony extensions we call "arms?" Oh sure, you hear about the thumb, but it would be nothing without these daddy-long-leg fingers, these music-playing, paintbrush-grasping sticks that are both set apart from us and connected to us. Of all the things about us, cluttering-up the world, certainly these veiny, freckled things are ours; they nearly never fail to do what we ask of them without us even having to ask.

Long before the digital revolution, these digits were creating an evolutionary furor all their own. The ten little puppies that I rattle on my keyboard to communicate to you are no small sausages in terms of biologically-formed tools. They are the killer app of anatomy: They make other tools possible.

No longer should these workhorses of humanity languish in media blackout. The cat polls are in, people, and your hands win for "Cats' Most Popular Part of You," hands down. It's not just the can-opener magic that they do, the knobs they turn, the doors they open. It's the kitty massages that your hands give, the under-chin rub, the behind-the-ear scratch. For this, a million years of evolution. From a cat's point of view, it was well worth it.

Around the world, most creatures enjoy a good pat or a scratch, from the whales in the sea to the bears in the forests. Of course most of these animals will never know the incredible gift of touch that people have to offer, due to obvious logistical problems.

Thankfully, no logistical problems should keep you from using your ten tiny friends on your cat. Liberal application of hands-on activities will make your cat's productivity grow and grow and grow.

4

In the Cat Zone: Home-Life How-to's That'll Stoke Your Cat's Efficiency Fire

Okay, so it's time to get psyched and to psyche-up your cat! This chapter will show you how to create a space in kitty's head and home that will get your feline fur-mine started hatching golden brain-eggs in no time. Are you ready for some hard-hitting, profit-making advice? Well then, simply take these steps with your cat and take your cat to the bank.

Toning Up for Time Management for Cats

Whatever level of stimulation and genius your cat may start at today, I want you to immediately start including two activities into your daily routine: Cat Adoration Times and Cat Play Therapy.

Proper Cat Adoration Practices

Cats are like water. By the time you feel thirsty, you are already dehydrated. Similarly, when a cat asks for affection, he is already running a relatively-serious affection deficit. Don't wait until you are thirsty or your cat asks for loving before you take a drink or pet your cat, respectively.

To extend the metaphor a little farther (than I should), remember, some say you need eight glasses of water each and every day. Similarly, you should work up to at least eight sessions of appreciating your cat, daily.

A well-adored cat is easy to recognize, just as a cat that lacks a full adoration schedule shows the silent tarnish of sullen neglect. Schedule Cat Adoration Times (C.A.T.s) regularly to ensure you completely adore your cat. These scheduled times can last anywhere from a few moments to hours on end. The important thing is that your cat be adored properly, with your full attention, and at every opportunity.

Cat Adoration Stations: A Necessity?

Considering ripping out walls or calling the architect in

order to set up a fancy new C.A.S., or Cat Adoration Station? Wait! Before you do, please remember that it's perfectly possible for you to learn appropriate cat adoration technique in your home as it currently stands. Try these prompts:

—Practice cat adoration at the same time every day. This will train your brain and your cat to proper adoration scheduling.

—Put on some relaxing music. Pavlov's Bells or something.

—Keep a Cat Adoration Time log. Some people do better when they have a record. This technique has done *wonders* for my litter box cleaning.

—Try using existing architecture. Chairs, cat trees, and the floor are all fine places for cat adoration as you contemplate an investment in a dedicated retrofit.

—If you must call an architect for dedicated C.A.S. space, use only those certified by the Feline Construction Board of America.

Cat Play Therapy

Everyone needs to stop thinking of playtime as off time. Play is actually the most important work you can do with your cat. Play is the place all good things are germinated and should always be your default activity if you ever find yourself wondering what to do next in your *Time Management for Cats* program, or otherwise.

Cats need a great deal of stimulation to stay in peak career form, but you will need to work up to it if your cat hasn't been worked-out in a while. Like any form of exercise, start with a wise number of regular workouts before you go running that 10K.

I can't tell you how to play with your cat. It is your job and duty to figure out what your cat likes and doesn't. And by the time you figure it out, he will have tired of whatever it is anyway and you will need to evolve it. Some people say this is because cats are finicky, but actually this early-onset disinterest is an essential part of the human-cat play interaction.

The reason a cat loses interest so fast is because his boredom is beating your boredom to the pass. In this way, the cat is making his best effort to keep *you*, the human, interested and engaged and to keep the play coming.

In order that you won't have to reinvent the cat entertainment wheel every few minutes, you need to develop a few themes to your play that can be combined in variation to keep kitty occupied. Beyond that, it's pretty much a matter of experimentation and catching your cat in the mood. The more play you do with your cat, the easier it will come for both of you. Eventually, the two of you will get so good you will be able to play in your sleep, or at least while one of you is sleeping.

Get Your Cat's Act Together

So your cat is all awake and ready to go but feeling just a tad scattered? Organization is really, *really* important. As you get started just remember that organizing your cat appears to be a simple matter, but there are hidden pitfalls that anyone who wants a well-organized cat needs to keep in mind.

Here is the problem: The first step to organization, as every professional organizer worth her drawer dividers knows, is to buy a notebook-style life organizer. And the very first step in messing up any effort at a newly-organized-you is to *not use* the organizer. Abandoned organizers are the leading cause of disorganization amongst the recently-organized, it's epidemic.

Sure, you can *buy* kitty an organizer. Get one with a cat on it, or a mouse, or a delicate, hand-drawn carrot. But all the organizers in the world stacked together in a massive at-a-glance mountain won't help kitty if he refuses to use it.

The question is not whether kitty can get past this debacle; it's whether *you* can. The organizer purchase is the very launch pad of the organization process, its disuse always the fatal derailment. But as counterproductive as it may feel, kitty's case will require that you "think outside the planner."

It all goes back to the client here, Kitty J. Kitty. We need to look at *his* needs and limitations, and there is just a fact of life standing in the way of our best efforts. The fact is this: Cats can't read and write. They haven't had all of the evolutionary opportunities we humans have enjoyed. Cats never found the leisure time to read, and they can't even hold a book. They may have opposable personalities, but they need opposable thumbs.

Still, it's not what you have but how you use it, and cats have certainly come a long way from their modest tree-home beginnings to enjoy the same trappings of worldly achievement as the most successful of people. Cats have managed to Make It in the human world, and with much less gray matter and gray hair than their *Homo sapiens* counterparts.

All this to say "go ahead" and get kitty an organizer if it makes you feel better. Anything to help you get past this obstacle to discover that organizing your cat actually is amazingly simple. If humans had so little clutter, people, organizing professionals would be out of a job.

Still, I don't want you to think you aren't getting your money's worth, so I have included a few organizing tips that will help put your cat's life into infinite order.

Quik Organizing Tips for Productive Cats

Tip #1: Remember to always keep catnip sealed and stored away from cats. There is no bigger waste of time and focus than when kitty breaks into your baggie of the c'nip and flops about in it until he passes out.

Tip #2: Place all cat furniture and props in easy-access positioning. Never store or stack your things on top of your cat's tower, dungeon, or scratching post, which could lead to Cat Anger Syndrome and other creative blockages.

Tip #3: Decorate to stimulate. Studies indicate that a cat's surroundings have a huge impact on his overall ability to achieve. A nice, running-mouse wallpaper could double or even triple his productivity!

Don't Let Your Cat Forget to Network

If everyone is up on their shots, small cat get-togethers can provide the kind of peer support that every working cat needs to get ahead. At cat networking events, don't forget to give everyone time to catch up with each other and enjoy a light refreshment before it's time to settle down and talk turkey.

Turning Cat Flow into Cash Flow

Time now to talk about the concept of flow. Flow may sound kind of mystical, but it is actually super-practical. Flow is a way of being in the world that, with a little direction from you, can lead your cat to the outer limits of his productivity.

Flow is nothing new to your cat, because the fact is cats are constantly in flow. Their reclined, relaxed bodies ooze forth flow like a puddle spreading outwards.

Without walls, cats flow forth into the world. Flow must be contained because we don't live in a cat's world. Risk-wise, today's cats live in something like the Dark Ages, where the odds for a long life plummet the minute Whiskers flows out the door.

On the other hand, however, your cat's flow may have poured right into the path of least resistance, perhaps causing tell-tale "flow marks" between his bed and the food bowl. That's because your cat needs a hobby. And better yet, a hobby that turns a profit, so the money will flow in. But profits aside, there is nothing like setting up and seeing your cat thrive in a new pass-time. He'll get that sparkle back in his eye, and that va-va-vigor for life will return.

Start today by scheduling Cat Flow Times. Go ahead, mark the date in kitty's organizer and make it official.

Scheduling Cat Flow Times

When should you schedule Cat Flow Times? Start by asking yourself, "When is the cat awake?" When your cat is not sleeping is precisely when you should schedule Cat

Flow Times.

During periods of wakefulness, it is very important that all the materials your cat needs for his chosen craft be set out for him in organized fashion. There is no sooner way to blow the flow than to have the tools of flow not available at Flow Time. You see, flow is all about tuning out the world and *living in the moment.*

Allow me to offer just a few words now on this concept of living or being "in the moment." I would like to meet the person who *isn't* living in the moment, because that seems like a neat trick. As far as I can tell, we have no choice but to live in the moment, but if we did have another choice, I would choose it. I live near an "in the moment" cult and these people tell me I'm not living in the moment. Because if I was living in the moment, I would sleep with them and their fellow, not-too-attractive, in-the-moment-cult people.

I don't think anyone can tell you that you aren't living in the moment. And if you have a cat, you have a four-footed anchor in the moment. Just don't let that anchor drag you down to the bottom of the sea of moments. Try to float in the surface of the moment. Show kitty how it's done, and soon he'll be dog-paddling in the moment good as Lassie.

Now, if your cat doesn't seem to naturally flow toward one activity or another, you will need to provide a lot of support and guidance to help him find one. If, for example, your cat won't even get up except to eat, you have a very bad case there. I suggest you immediately go back and start a seven-day crash course regimen of Cat Play Therapy. Play will help stretch your cat's flow muscles, improving flow stamina. Only after play comes easily and naturally should you start to again incorporate Flow Times into your program.

Whether he gets there through work or play, when your cat's in his flow, you'll know. Notice the incomparable feline focus, the delightfully malicious twinkle in his little alien predator eye slats. Aren't you glad now that you aren't eight inches tall and smelling like prey? Yes, the cat would be a formidable foe if our two sizes were switched. But they are not, and human beings can help transform kitty's killing instincts into make-a-killing instincts with just a little time and commitment.

Finally, I must make one more essential point on this topic: Never forget to put any and all tools of Cat Flow Time away *immediately* afterward. This way your cat will not grow accustomed to them and ignore them at every opportunity.

The Cat Home Office

Every cat dreams of a home office. As he whiles away the day under the bed, on the bed, under the covers, on your pillow—or wherever, chances are your cat is wishing he was working away at a cozy little home office.

The home office is to modern cats what communist utopia was to the working class wretch of yesteryear. It is long mornings sipping catpuccino between client calls. It is being there for family when they need your cat self, except on those occasions when there is some hairy deadline at which times the family units become intensely annoying—but that isn't all the time. It is working on your own cat schedule, being your own cat boss, and taking off for the food bowl any old time you feel like it.

In other words, it's a dream that will never withstand the reverse-clean-room test of reality. A cat home office would have trouble holding a candle to life as cats' presently know it. But that doesn't stop your cat from *dreaming*. After all, he sleeps so damn much of the time; dreams just come with the territory.

If your cat has been bugging you to build him a home office, by all means, do it.

Now some may say building a home office before your cat has work is putting the cart before the horse. These are no doubt the same people who say you must have a year's living saved up before quitting your job to go freelance or that you must do a lot of informational interviews before switching careers, etc. These careful plodders just love to give you long, time-consuming tasks to undertake before you get to the good stuff. I have never been big on this type of advice. My motto is "Take the plunge and let the chipped teeth fall as they may."

If your cat says he wants a home office even if he has no idea what to do with it, well, I say give it to him. Cats need that kind of instant gratification to move forward in the world.

Once you create a great place for your cat to go after his morning coffee, the rest is easy. Surrounded by the proper filing system, pencil sharpener, and home computer, it is only a matter a time before your cat's great ideas start flowing. One more important point here: If you happen to catch your cat catnapping at his new workstation, do not disturb him. This should be his "safe" place. If you awaken him here, he may turn his back on his home office forever, and then where will you be?

Is Your Cat Ready To Freelance?

Sure, you daydream of a freewheeling, freelance life for your cat. But is kitty ready for the responsibility of being chief cook and bottle washer? Really, *really* ready? Ready to "live lean" in those tough "start-up" years when most new cat endeavors go "belly-up?"

Should your cat freefall into freelance like a sky-diving chipmunk on speed? Or should your favorite fur ball stay in the slow lane to self-employment success? Take this quiz to find out:

1. In your cat's most energetic, "up" moments, s/he:

a. Is walking to the food bowl.
b. Is walking on the ceiling.

2. When at play, your cat reveals:

a. Its innate, aggressive will to get ahead through feathericide.
b. Its vast inner pools of boredom for you and your kind.

3. When left alone all day, your kitty opts for:

a. A 12-hour sleep marathon with no breaks.
b. A bona fide effort to make something, ruin something, or at least stir.

4. Which one is your cat?

a. Finds his/her own "projects."
b. Better at following than leading.

5. So far, the tips in this book have:

a. Transformed kitty's life into a more productive, satisfied existence.
b. Turned your cat into a strange reclusive creature who runs when he sees you.

If you picked answer A for numbers 2, 4, & 5, your cat is ready for the plunge. A freelance career could start as early as now, just read on to find opportunities for smart, self-employed cats.

If you picked the other way, don't worry too much. Freelancing isn't for everyone. Someone has to be the wage slave, and that someone is your cat. Read on to learn all the exciting careers available for today's quality team-player cat.

5

What Color Is Your Shredded Parachute?
Vocational First-Aid for Cats

Finding a career for cats is as easy as asking the following two questions:

A. What is my cat "good" at, and

B. How can I exploit it mercilessly?

When looking at careers for cats or whoever, there is a little piece of fantasy I remember from a bumper sticker:

Do what you love and the money will follow you.

I like this idea, but I have a slightly different version:

Do what you love and the debt collectors will follow you.

Any serious book—or chapter—on cat vocations would be errant not to point out the cold truth about cat careers: Today's cat job market shows extreme limitations. But I wouldn't be too discouraged about the current unemployment rate against these non-human job seekers. There are signs of more cat job opportunities all the time, with some cats landing great deals as chain-store spokes-animals and the like.

If your cat is not suitable for a job in the competitive cat-product industry, perhaps he could get a job as a bookshop cat, the number-two cat job in the nation, or any of the many other jobs I suggest in this and upcoming chapters. In the mean time, I strongly encourage you to get your cat started with small projects around the home. Remember, one doesn't *have* to hold a paying job to be a productive member of a household or society, although it bloody sure helps.

Then after basic skills are honed, it's time to toot that little kitty horn. Don't let your feline genius languish in non-renown. Whether it's a blog, brochure, or resume, your cat needs a little marketing help if he wants to hit a kitty home run.

Top Ten Cat Resume No-Nos:

The resume is the dewclaw of any job hunt. As the above subheading sufficiently describes, here are few things to leave out of your cat's resume:

Nicknames: They may be cute, but save them for the cover letter.

Wacky Sports Metaphors: Some of this is unavoidable, but try to keep the shuttlecocks in their can.

Lies: Fibs and fudges, yes, but there's a whisker-thin line that one mustn't cross.

Cute Fonts, Clip Art & Colored Paper: A no-nonsense document positively *stinks* of success.

Claw Marks & Signs of Shredding: Reveals poor impulse control. Ditto for signs of sleeping on the resume.

Too Much Info: Keep it to a page by weaning irrelevant or embarrassing life chapters.

Too Little Info: Got nothing to write about? Volunteering can help gain valuable experience and resume content. Cat volunteers today make a world of difference in senior homes, the prisons, and anywhere they can share their special brand of service.

Never hesitate to weave the names of your cat's household chores into impressive sounding job titles like: Chief Carpet Inspector, Head of Door Security, Pest Control Management Specialist, Senior Paper Weight, etc.

A Note on Careers & Cats

Don't know what your cat is "good" at? Career ambiguity can strike anyone at anytime and often hits the most creative and intelligent among us the hardest.

I have lived with more than my share of career ambiguity, not so much for myself as for my longtime boyfriend. Nearly everyone he knows has tried to find a career for him. Most only give it passing thought, but others, like his father, seem to make finding a job for Hank a life's work in and of itself.

Yes, it's time for a personal antidote, I mean anecdote.

Hank's dad Gus once called me shortly after I had purchased my first car, a sick-green rust-pustuled pick-up with a permanent sneer in its driver's-side fender where an earlier owner had hydroplaned smack into a phone pole some years prior. Adding to the charm of this, the first vehicle to ever have my name on its title, was the unparalleled experience of an interior door latch that didn't work on the driver's side (you had to unroll the window to let yourself out), and a window glass on the passenger side that was booby trapped to plunge deep into the door if the passenger so much as cracked it open.

Dad's idea: Start an airport shuttle service in our "new" truck.

As if fated, Dad's other life plans for Hank suffered

similar design flaws but almost always involved a haircut early in the process. Through this type of exchange I learned two things about career advice. First and foremost to never give it to my boyfriend, who has enough stored-up somewhere for ten lifetimes. And secondly, that advice in career choice is a futile activity. It's like trying to save someone else's soul. You can lead a horse to water, but you can't make him get baptized.

To uncover the true calling that each one of us was born-to is a lifetime journey, and largely a process of elimination. A career quest is not so much finding what one *wants* to do, but rather avoiding what one *hates* to do while still keeping the air hole sufficiently above surface.

Cat Career Choices

Ultimately, you cannot choose a career for anyone but yourself. So there is no need to fret over what career path your cat should get started on. All you can do is leave the college catalogs lying around. You can't force your cat to go to class.

Sure, you can do the exercises in this book, and make suggestions, and encourage and coddle and cajole. But at some point your cat is either going to enroll at the cat talent agency or he is going to go under the bed to get away from you. The cat has a lifetime of lazing around to fall back on and remember, Rome wasn't built in a blink. So back off, give kitty some space. You don't make the sun come up either, you know.

Remember this, and this is key: Your cat's hard-wired purpose in life is to remind you that your powers as a human only go so far. You may boss your family around and your employees. All the wait staffs at all your favorite restaurants may wince when you walk in. You may make careers rise and fall at the day job. Your office may be known as star-maker central. More careers may have been conceived on your casting couch than you care to count. But your cat could give a big fat yawn for any of it.

Cat doesn't do what you say, haven't you figured that out by now? So take a big chill pill. You need to learn something about charming your cat's socks off. Only then will you have the influence and savoir-faire to suggest that six-week certificate course in cat chair massage.

Profile in Success: "Stop Eating the Boa!" Case Study of a Cat Entrepreneur

Melissa "Foxy" O'Hara offers a new service that you have to see to appreciate. Imagine cats traipsing about in their birthday suits in various luxurious settings, caught repeatedly in the act of posing, primping, and giving that "come hither and pet me, dammit" look. Now put it on film forever, and you have the latest, greatest thing for animal companions since the catnip cigar.

The new art of cat boudoir photography hasn't caught up with all regions of the nation just yet, but it is a growing form that is more popular than you would think, although still a specialist's game to be sure. As a seasoned cat boudoir photographer in L.A., the birthplace of cat boudoir photography, Foxy has seen just about everything and knows all the tricks.

"It's not as easy as it would seem," she shared after completing a stressful shoot involving a litter of hairless Sphynxes, a blazing fireplace, and a faux bearskin rug. "Cats love to lounge about acting sexy, but strictly on their own terms."

While getting some cats to just sit still is a problem, Foxy's toughest challenge is just getting the look she wants from the cat.

"Some cats give up that soft-focus bedroom expression to a complete stranger easier than others."

Then there's the perennial problem of cats and feather boas. "That's probably my biggest issue on the job," she confided. "I go through miles of boas. I have to buy them by the big giant roll."

Although most Americans seem largely unaware that cat boudoir photography exists as a service, Foxy O'Hara says she is always in demand in cat-loving L.A., where cats sleazing it up in Victoria's Cat's Secrets and high heels is not a sign of advanced decadence but rather the greatest, latest thing since, well, the catnip cigar.

What Your Cat's Playthings
Say About Their Career Path.

Match your cat's favorite activities with a new future career. If your cat likes to (blank), he may have a future in/as a (blank). Here are a few examples to get you started.

-If your cat likes to attack coins on the floor, he may have a future in finance!

-If he "shreds" paper you leave out, he may be a "natural" attorney.

-If he climbs trees, he may have a future as a lumberjack or phone-repair cat.

-If he likes to dig and kick in the litter box, you may have a born soccer star!

-If your cat likes to stare at himself in a mirror, consider cosmetic counter sales.

-If your cats likes to "talk," he may have a future in politics.

-If your cat likes to sleep, he could be a peace officer.

-If your cat likes to make you bleed, he may have the heart of a professional wrestler.

-If tearing your furniture to shreds is his thing, you may have a future trend analyst.

-If your cat <u>loves to play with feathers,</u> he might make a <u>good ostrich farmer.</u>

-If your cat's talent is to <u>break stuff,</u> you may have yourself a <u>born rock 'n' roll star!</u>

A Small Disclaimer

In spite of everything we know about extracting value from your cat, there remains of course an extremely slim possibility that your cat may display limited career talent of any kind whatsoever. Some cats are only "good at" being adorable, and even that only at intervals. If you find yourself tied to this type of creature, it may be time to ask yourself: Is it enough to be adorable?

You won't be the first to wonder at this quandary.

6

Seven Habits of Highly Effective Cats
And Other Problems You May Run Into

Habits. We all have them. Good habits. Bad habits. Naturally, I was attracted to a program that prescribed them. I started by asking, what exactly are cat habits?

I racked my brain. Before long, I realized that cats don't really have habits so much as they have instincts. But why get caught up in semantics? Here are seven cat habits-slash-instincts (slash, slash) and how you can use them to turn your cat's life into one long continuous improvement process.

The Ceaseless Habit of Culinary Passion:

Have you ever noticed that nothing gets your cat "up and

at 'em" faster, day or night, than the prospect of a new meal or sometimes even just the *hope* of a treat? Why, I set out some treat just last night, and as I did, Brody burst around the corner at a surprising speed and did not slow until his head was in full contact with the bowl. I had forgotten how quick he can be when duly motivated.

The shadow side of this passion/habit is cats' high susceptibility to becoming treat junkies, hanging around their pusher/source where the substance is immediately mainlined (usually, the fridge). I'm afraid Brody is indeed such an addict, spending hours daily soliciting for his very own version of black gold heroin: powdered nutritional yeast. When he gets his fix, he gobbles it down with such vigor and without any of the sharing with his "brother" that occurs around the food. It proves to me that cats can indeed feel greed, and if that doesn't give them an edge in the current economy, nothing will.

This promising passion for food is a heretofore undeveloped career field for cats, thanks in no small part to their longtime ban from food establishments.

The Ever-Present Habit of Watchfulness:

The main habit of a cat is to watch the world. When awake and alert, and maybe even as they sleep, they are constantly scanning their environment with their ears, eyes, nose, whiskers, and possibly other body parts we don't know about yet.

There is no better way to know if my apartment is under attack than to keep an eye on my cats. Once there was a fire in my building, and the cats reacted to it long before any human being came around to inform us of this fact. I know someone whose cat woke him up one night when his car was about to be stolen just outside. Maybe cats can't bark like dogs, but their sharper senses and stealthier response to danger offer a different, more subtle kind of "alarm service."

Any kind of work that requires watchfulness is going to tap into this natural ability. Look for positions in security (e.g. bodyguards) and law enforcement.

The Adorable-Companion Factor:

One habit cats never have to think about is the habit of being so damn adorable. Cats are basically pelt-bearing love essence, kibble-to-love conversion engines. They're capable of great and true friendship, a skill seemingly beyond the capacity of many human beings in today's rush-on-by world.

But it goes a lot farther than that: Cats are *proven* health therapists. Studies show they can lower people's blood pressure on the spot. As long as your cat doesn't get caught up in the rat race him or herself, their capacity for caring could provide the competitive edge to get ahead in mental health, organized religion, the courts, and waiting rooms everywhere.

Inherent Beauty: The Habit of Looking Good

Face it: Sleek, slinky felines have it all over most people looks-wise. Cats always manage to be so hip and cool all the time. That's why people love to wear cat fur (most of it fake, thank goddess), and you always see pictures of cats selling the priciest, most classy stuff. Cats' charismatic power over people points to a career in fashion, the arts, entertainment, or politics.

Physical Fitness: The Habit to Use It, Not Lose It

Here's another field cats stand-out in. Cats are badass athletes who can run and jump, tackle and eviscerate with the best of them! That's why you see so many cat mascots and teams named after cats.

Cats aren't just physically superior, some of them are crazy enough to need to prove it. In fact, cats' competitive nature and determination to win may at times drive them a little too far, past the point of healthy pursuit. Like Brody, who took a deep feline pride in surmounting our ever-increasing backyard barricades in a series of escalating Houdini-like feats (or was it Evel Knievel?) that suggested levitation.

Otherwise, cats are generally good about taking care of themselves, and can be our role models here. All those cleaning contortions and sundry stretches make them natural yoga instructors, personal trainers, and all-around spiritual gurus. Cats are nearly perfect beings—as far as carnivores go. That doesn't always equate to a good income, though.

The Playful Habit:

Cats always know that a little cat and mousing takes the edge off and breaks up the monotony. Also, it keeps you at top form for when pred or prey drop by for "lunch." How can play become work and work play? It's an age-old question. Try studying something fun, then start a consultancy.

The Hygiene Habit:

Cats constantly clean themselves. Unfortunately, they use their tongues. You can't very well have your cat become an industrial or household cleaner, but don't rule out a consultancy in the high-paying personal-hygiene industries. Beauty salons do a land-office business in my neighborhood. You can't get anything to eat for miles around, but you can get your feet patinaed at any of two-dozen unique and well-patronized establishments.

Now a word about one of cat's rare bad habits…

Sleep: Too Much of a Good Thing?

As insomnia levels in humans rise, with more and more products available all the time to help us sleep, it is with heavy, red, sleep-deprived eyes that we look jealously at a creature for whom it is as easy to sleep as it is to scratch, stretch, and yawn. And so it is with some trepidation that I bring up the topic of sleep and cats, for clearly to mess with a critter's sleep habits is the worst sort of Pandora's Box. Yet any serious discussion of cats and productivity cannot occur without significant mention of the topic of sleep.

Cats act as if sleep is the most productive activity of them all. They go about it with a discipline and care that artists of all bents can only dream of. They live for sleep, and lightly. You won't catch them chatting about it at cocktail parties.

I, too, once lived for sleep. But eventually, even I had to graduate from college. When I did, I learned that there were things to live for beyond the pillow and the blankee. It's possible that the cat can also be brought around to this point of view, even if we haven't been able to duplicate proof in the lab.

The key, I think, is to meet the cat on its own terms. Admittedly, a 15-hour sleep schedule equals a well-rested cat. The problem is that what kitty accomplishes in the few remaining hours of the day can hardly justify such extended knockout naps. Through reason alone can you wean your slug muffin away from a life spent two-thirds in the ether.

If you can get the cat on-board in the rationale department, the rest of the job is simple, if time-consuming. For the real trick to getting your cat to stay awake is to *keep* him awake, and how you do that is up to you. Just be warned, after a day or three of attempting to keep kitty up, you may start to lose faith in this project, or perhaps even in the whole idea of cat time management itself. If your faith does flag, take strength, for it most certainly is a sign that you are headed for a breakthrough.

For in the darkest hour, as you get stuck under the bed trying to awaken a retractable, sleep-deprived creature that resembles a demon from Dante more than your sweet pet of yesterday, and you begin to think that not only have you wasted two days of your life and perfectly good money on this book, but that you have wasted your WHOLE life, and squandered ALL your resources on NOTHING, that is precisely the moment, as Muffin opens an artery in the all-consuming blackness, when you will be on the very outer lip of the verge of mastering *Time Management for Cats*.

So hang in there! And if by some bizarre twist of fate, *Time Management for Cats* does not bestow its wisdom on you at this moment or shortly thereafter, perhaps what you need is the "full immersion" experience of a visit with your cat to your local *Time Management for Cats* time-share spa.

7

Permanent Success Road Show:
Cat Life Makeovers That Work

At this point in the book, I think we all could use a little inspiration. That's right; it's time for the Real Life Success Stories.

Real Cat Life Stories of
Cats Who Made It

Every book like this needs at least a handful of true accounts to prove the author's point, so let me tell you all I know about cats who Made It in four fields: The Arts, Destination Travel, Politics, and Science.

Art Cats, Lit Cats, Tour Cats

Cats and creative expression go together like bleeding

and band-aids, so naturally there exists no shortage of cats in the world of great art. Here, as in other fields, the most successful cats—the ones who have truly made their marks—enjoyed symbiotic relationships with their humans.

Every artist from Picasso on down has employed a cat model at one time or another. Joan Brown, the first American artist to "write-off" her cats on her federal income taxes, went so far as to make the cat her alter ego on canvas, a theme explored in many wonderful paintings like the half-cat, half-Joan self portrait, lovingly titled *Harmony*.

Writers also have chosen to associate with cats—and be associated with them. If you keep an eye out, you'll notice that writers often can't resist weaving cats into their stories or, in the very least, posing in publicity photos with their cat friends. Don't think these clever authors and artists aren't putting their cat's mystique to work for them. And you can, too, if you can just figure out "*how?*"

As great as the cats of great artists are, there exists today an island cat community that has shattered the boundaries of good service to their literary owner, even decades after his untimely death. I am of course referring to Ernest Hemingway's famous multi-toed cats, whose descendents today provide a living monument to their author—and a newsworthy PR tool for his estate. I understand this boundary-breaking arrangement has its critics, and Hemingway's kitties have been dragged in and out of court in recent years. Nevertheless, Papa's cats remain extremely devoted, creating a large population of happy "greeters" at the author's Key West digs.

Their polydactyl brand of cat hospitality is rivaled only by the cats of Rome, who also earn handsome livings from the cat-tourist trade. And really, what destination wouldn't benefit from happy cats lounging about? Imagine Persians passed-out by the pools at Hearst Castle, mini-panthers pacing at the Alcazar, Abyssinians sunning on the sphinx, tiny tigers tussling at the Taj Mahal. There is almost no end to the possibilities of cat tourism, tastefully executed, of course.

Funny Cat, Drama Cat: Feline Film Roles

Cats as a species have a reputation of being hard to work with in Hollywood. This injustice is compounded by the fact that most cat film roles are schlocky and cartoonish. These problems will likely persist until cats infiltrate into more powerful jobs, like directing and producing.

Cat parts are almost exclusively comedic, usually playing "the straight man" to some incredible goofball, like would-be world dominator Dr. Evil (Mike Myers) and Mister Bigglesworth (a hairless Sphynx), the pair of laughable baddies from the Austin Powers movies.

Comedy is one thing, and then there is *serious* cat acting.

Topping the list of quality cat roles is the role of "Cat" in *Breakfast at Tiffany's* (1961). Here, alongside Audrey Hepburn, Cat brings home all the poignant results that occur when cats take part in important plot points. Played by the lovely orange tabby, Orangey, his performance won a well-deserved PATSY, the animal equivalent of an Oscar.

Orangey was already the very first feline PATSY winner, for his earlier work in the noir comedy *Rhubarb* (1952), about a cat who inherits a baseball team. He shared his PATSY glory that year with fellow-winner Francis the mule, a perennial favorite who dominated the PATSYs five out of six years running in the 1950s. The winner list is notably light on felinity and more heavily populated with dog, bear and pony shows. Other animal actors awarded include a rat, a raccoon, and a pigeon. Sadly, the PATSYs are no longer officially celebrated.

Another good cat part was the role of "General Sterling Price," cat of Rooster Cogburn in *True Grit* (1969). Cats in the Wild West? Heck, yeah! John Wayne earned his only Oscar playing this tough cat-loving curmudgeon, another reason cats everywhere *love* John Wayne. Beef kitty stew; it's what's for dinner.

Also notable, the leading kitty role of "Tonto cat" in *Harry & Tonto* (1974). Here the headline character, an apartment cat from the Big Apple, braves eviction and heads out on the great American road trip with his Harry, an aging human, on the other end of the leash.

Sadly, these quality and ground-breaking cat roles reflecting true-life cathood haven't seen a cinematic match in decades. (Please cat-film lovers, pounce on me gently with what I may have overlooked.)

On a brighter note, and for all the naysayers that say cats are too "difficult" for live theater, some brave souls have just brought the great role of "Cat" to Broadway in *Breakfast at Tiffany's*! For once and for all, let these pioneering feline thespians prove to the world: Cats and theater can mix!!

Science's Star Kitty: Quantum the Cat

Although naturally drawn to the arts, cats have not been completely absent from the sciences. By far the most famous of all egghead cats was Schrodinger's cat, who caused a major fuss in Quantum Physics when he slashed wide-open the theory of Superposition. (Superposition theory suggests that a thing is anywhere and everywhere in the universe until the observer actually pins it down to one location, which explains the state of affairs in my apartment all too well.)

Who better than a cat to sink their fangs into humans' deepest held scientific beliefs about the nature of matter and energy on the subatomic and atomic levels? Yes, Quantum the cat caused quite an upset when he came on the physics scene back in 1935 in Erwin Schrodinger's essay: *Die gegenwartige Situation in der Quantenmechanik*, (*The*

Present Situation in Quantum Mechanics).

From what I gather, Schrodinger's cat entered a metal box in order to mess with Schrodinger, who was probably spending too much time with his Quantum Physics problems and not enough time with his cat. Shutting his cat self inside the box with a deadly suicide device, cute little Quantum allowed enough time to pass where poor old Schrodinger no longer knew if his kitty's hummer was humming, or if he'd sung his last meow.

(Over the years, said suicide device has been anything from a complicated radioactive isotope thingy or a vile of arsenic to an old moldy bowl of mac & cheese— something that may or may not kill kitty. It is the uncertainly of it all that matters, as any cat person knows.)

Understand, this was a maddening situation for a physicist, because Schrodinger is forced by the laws of physics to conclude that his cat is both alive and dead. Some time later, after a long nap, Quantum the cat emerged, unscathed and ready for a treat, having perplexed the best minds of his generation.

Now, Schrodinger and his MC-squared buddies weren't crazy about the implications of this experiment, but they couldn't deny that his cat had a point. Because, you see, everyone knows a cat can't really be alive and dead at the same time, but it took a cat to prove it.

More importantly, the experiment made a key point

about what humans know from experience, versus what they know from all their brain-work. Scientists always want to downplay the power of experience and be oh-so-objective and logical. But the cat says, "Wait a minute, Spock. Don't bail on experience and get all lost up inside that big clunky mind shaft over your pie-hole." Because being alive and being dead are what's real, and anything that you think is both alive and dead should smell a little fishy.

One of the more progressive aspects of Schrodinger's cat experiment is that no cat had to die, or even risk dying, for it. You see, Schrodinger and his cat pioneered the animal *thought* experiment. I would like to encourage more scientists (and their cats) to conduct animal thought experimentation instead of actual animal experimenting, which is *oh so* 16th century.

PolitiKitty: Socks in the Whitehouse

In the modern era, cats have gone so far as to make it to the White House. But what the First Cats have done once they Made It there reveals the entrenched obstacles that remain for catus politicus—aka Politikitty.

It shouldn't be any surprise that the president who broke the cat barrier at 1600 Pennsylvania Avenue was that freedom-loving, beard-wearing, controversy-generating character known as Abraham Lincoln. I bet old Honest Abe couldn't wait to let his little pal Tabby loose to shred

Van Buren's loveseat and the like.

The next presidents to keep a feline on staff included Rutherford B. Hayes and Theodore Roosevelt, not exactly pussies themselves in either domestic policy or foreign relations. But the next really notable First Cat to impact national politics was Calvin Coolidge's favorite cat, Tiger, who was nearly never absent from his official place in the cabinet—looped about the president's neck—where he tirelessly consulted on all presidential matters large and small.

Not every president's cat is made of such political fiber. The truth is, we have yet to see a truly empowered First Cat who can capture this nation's imagination and toy with it, for the sake of real-life results.

Certainly, being First Cat was a mixed bag for Socks Clinton, the black and white short hair from Arkansas who became the White House's first modern celebrity cat of the paparazzi era. The privileges and responsibilities of holding the highest cat office in the land could not have been easy for this simple southern kitten named for the white spots on his feet.

Thrust suddenly into the flash-drenched limelight, Socks suffered the errors and manipulations of many outsiders who break into the power-core only to find themselves under the microscope and inside the fish bowl. Like many a social pioneer before him, this boundary breaker was not entirely in control of his own destiny or public image.

There is no pussy-footing around the fact that even with two terms in office, Socks caused a lot of excitement but got not a lot accomplished for the cat agenda. Afterwards, though, Socks seemed to step out from behind the Clinton shadow, marshalling a few parades, winning regional "Cat of the Year" awards, etc. Everyone knows it's much easier being a *former* First Cat.

Socks cracked open *some* drawers of opportunity for catkind. The next generation of politicians' cats need to break wide-open the drawers of opportunity, kick out their contents, and start making real progress for the species.

There are so many areas where charismatic, articulate cats could make a real difference. Today, battles are being fought and decided about cats and housing, food safety, disaster planning, population control and cat euthanasia ("kitty death row"), the feral community, and so much more. Only through organization, education, and political involvement will these things improve for cats. Right now, we have a long way to go before we live in anything approaching the cat-human utopia that is the promise of the cat-human bond, at least on the national level.

But as uninspired as the national political picture has been for cats and their people, there is good reason to keep hope alive. Mastering *Time Management for Cats* means nothing less than finding a new feline fuel source for 21ˢᵗ century cat social change at every level.

So are you ready to plug-in to your very own private, clean power plant on paws? In my next section, I'll reveal the final secret I've discovered to turning *Time Management for Cats* into a reality beyond your cat's wildest dreams.

How the Author's Cats Are Already Working for You

There is one more Real Life Success Story I have to share with you, my own success story. I'm about to reveal the biggest secret of all that I have found to successful *Time Management for Cats*.

Here is the secret: Your cats may *already be* working for you! Mine are. Allow me to explain.

A while ago, I received a call from a friend in London. She is a professional human psychic who, due to market trends, wanted to try her invisible hand at pet communication. To wit, she asked for some minimal information about my cats and proceeded to contact them paranormally from half a planet away.

The report of her exchange with my various cats, alive and dead, arrived in my email days later. The results floored me. Here I was wracking my brain to find a profitable hobby for Brody and Herman Panther, and all along they were already hard at work on the most important job of all. You see, according to my psychic friend, my cats were working diligently on the very book manuscript you are now reading!

That's right, I would not kid you about this. *Time Management for Cats* is a human-cat collaboration of the highest order. I for one am open-minded enough to entertain this possibility, or at least be entertained by it. I cannot however prove it by the high scientific standards I've set for *Time Management for Cats*. I do not *know* if she actually contacted my cats, or if the boys are really working on the book. But ever since I received this information, I have a whole new approach to completing my manuscript.

When it isn't going well, I simply ask for more help from my cats. I say, "Better get to work and stop procrastinating or someone will steal your idea." And when I hit a dry spell and have to set it down, I know that Brody and Herman will take up the slack, whether it's through shredding old drafts or simply "sleeping on" a segment or chapter. And if, per chance, the world doesn't embrace *Time Management for Cats* the way it should, well, I can now easily blame it on my cats. And that, my friend, is golden.

Taking Your Cat Success Show on the Road

Once you experience even just a modicum of success, it's time to consider taking your show on the road. A successful career is nice, but a career in success is lucrative beyond even your cat's most flagrant fantasies. By packaging your success formula to eager audiences, you and your cat will hardly have to work much anymore. And who wants to work so damn hard all the time anyway? Not your cat, that's for sure.

8

Your Cat Can Drive You Crazy: Advanced Advice for Applied TMC

Time and space have always gone together. You can't conquer one without controlling the other. A drip-proof schedule doesn't really go with flabby housekeeping and sloppy cat fat.

Today's sophisticated cats face many of the exact same problems their people face, but without the assistance of industry experts and an entire publishing genre to slim their wastes and purge their clutter. So little is written to bridge the gap between human self-help and cats' that I feel obliged to include a few award-winning articles I've written that at least scratch the surface of these essential life-quality topics.

Fit or Cat?
Solutions Toward a Cat Fat Problem

Like many Americans, I woke up a while back to the fact that my household has a looming weight problem. It just so happens that my family's extra pounds are carried around by my cat.

I never imagined in a million years my cat would get fat. In my mind, he was the scrappy kitten I plucked from the SPCA, a spring-action featherweight who could stalk and pounce with the best of them. I could still imagine feeling the ribs of this, my ideal cat, long after my actual cat's ribs had been covered in a layer of what I can only bring myself to admit is pure muscle.

Then one day, I had to face the fact that whatever was blocking the sunlight under my cat was attached to him. Imagine my horror when I uncovered what can only be called waddles of hanging flesh protruding from his former cat six-pack. After discovering this new appendage, I could no longer justify my cat's image as the hungry alley urchin in my mind. I had to see that my "little" Herman Panther was well on his way to being fat, if he wasn't there already.

There had been signs that he was approaching -- and passing -- his ideal weight. His nickname, the Fur Brick, might have been a clue.

He had always looked compact and strong, but his toughness had grown a little ... round. Who was I kidding? He had become a huge tube, a black caterpillar with legs. Thanks to his bruiser proportions, Herman looks as if he can kick serious butt. This is not likely, thanks to a personality more like a doofus, a coot in cat form.

So I could no longer ignore the fact that my cat was getting fat. After all, people would tell me all the time when they saw him. It's amazing how many friends and relatives felt perfectly comfortable commenting about his size and even scolding me for his eating habits.

Sure, he had a few extra pounds. But on one Internet cat list where I sought advice, I was lambasted so thoroughly for my cat's weight, you would think I had spent the past five years force-feeding him bon-bons until he couldn't squeeze through the cat door.

OK, he was tipping the scales at 20 pounds, but as I told everyone else, he's big boned. He could shed a few pounds, yes, but he wasn't being asked to try out for World's Fattest Cat Contest -- not yet, anyway.

Well, it turns out that even a few pounds overweight is bad for a cat's health, I learned, so I took the first logical step: I switched from super-triple-X premium regular cat food to super-triple-X premium cat food "slim." It only cost a little more to get fewer calories per piece of kibble, and the beast stopped expanding, at least. If only it were that simple for millions of overweight humans.

Now, slim cat food is only part of the answer, because

Herman also needed more activity. And when we moved to a larger place, he shed a few pounds -- for a while. But just like for people, watching a cat's weight can be a lifetime preoccupation. And, just like for people, a cat's weight can balloon during stressful periods, such as when they don't get enough of your time and attention.

I've noticed that Herman often goes to the food bowl when he feels bad (like after our other cat has jumped him or when he's not allowed out) or even if he's just bored. The professional advice for an overweight cat is to take the food away except at a set feeding time, but I have yet to resort to this measure. This solution would no doubt lead to more problems in my house. My other cat, Brody, has no weight problem but must have a bowl of food that is half full available at all times in order to feel at ease because, apparently, he grew up during his own version of the Great Depression.

So far we've managed to keep Herman down to a healthy size through play, love and triple-X slim. At the Fur Brick's last vet visit, the doctor confirmed it. Even at a lead-ingot-like 17 pounds, he passed the examination (surprisingly, considering he was there because he'd slipped and "flown" off our one-story porch).

The doctor felt Herman's tough underbelly and announced: "Herman's not fat, he's pure muscle."

I couldn't have been more pleased if he had been talking about me!

Fang Shui: The Art of Rearranging
Your Whole Life for Your Cat

Feng Shui, the ancient Chinese practice of creating a positive living space, has been hugely popular in the U.S. While these unusual theories guiding good living may be esoteric, the basic concept hits home with Americans who've always known that the best response to life's deep-seated problems is to redecorate.

However, cat owners who would like to try a little Feng Shui may hit a few snags, as I did, when attempting to apply the concepts to their own homes. Ancient Chinese wisdom may rule your roost, but my housekeeping is dictated by a couple of fur dragons on paws. What determines the order of my furnishings is based more on something I call Fang Shui.

Feng Shui: *The art of finding happiness by rearranging your home based on ancient Chinese tenets.*

Fang Shui: *The art of finding happiness by rearranging your entire life for your cat.*

FENG V. FANG: Let me start by noting that cats are not born enemies of Feng Shui, which actually approves of cats and other companion animals because they "stir up the chi." Chi is the life force that flows through a place, and Feng Shui, as far as I can tell, is all about managing its flow. You don't want the chi to stagnate, nor do you want it to rush through your pad too fast. Cats in their normal day-to-day activities help keep the chi moving around, and that, Martha Stewart, is a good thing.

However, other Feng Shui advisories seem to preclude a catted environment. I am forced to conclude that Feng Shui folks never actually shared their cave with a couple of fang-faced chi-wranglers. For example, I am uneasy with suggestions to put fresh flowers in key locations, which is said to boost your health or aid your family. Anywhere I put fresh flowers that isn't out of reach of los gatos guarantees only one outcome: a huge wet mess when they are knocked over. Does this qualify as "stirring up the chi"?

Similarly, thriving plants on one's work desk are said by Feng-ies to make your career thrive. I wonder, however, what plants with bunches of cat-chewed, dying leaves portend. Like the flowers, all my plants are placed where the cats can't reach them. Fang Shui in action.

WATER SPORTS: Gold fish are another questionable Feng Shui prescription. The goldfish is said to absorb their owner's bad energy, and if you have a real bad day the fish might even croak. I figure every day would be a bad day for the poor fish with my cats tormenting it. A more likely cause of death would be ulcers, heart attack, or a direct hit.

However, cats and Feng Shui don't always have to clash. Flowing water is good Feng Shui, and my cats love that idea. Herman Panther is so gaga for the plumbing, at any hour he can be found in the tub staring at the pipe, waiting for the elusive water creature to slither out. Turn the faucet on and his paw becomes a water-slaughtering machine, pounding the slippery stream into chop suey.

The Maine Coon cat also enjoys water play. He stands with his front feet in his water bowl, lifts a forepaw and shakes it, blessing any nearby ankles. While I like the idea of getting a peaceable table fountain (good Feng), I fear that I would come home one day to find the thing bone-dry and gasping, the house flooded, and the cats collapsed nearby (bad Fang).

MORE CAT ARRANGING: I have to admit, Feng Shui principals are over my head and beyond my capacity. In my crowded quarters, rearrangement to accommodate the chi is largely out of the question. I have about six square feet of surface space that is not traversed, spelunked, or rappeled by my cats (at least not on my watch, I occasionally find evidence of feline forays into even these off-limit places).

These surfaces are regularly inundated by receipts, notes, spare change, half sticks of gum and sundry minutiae that find their way in the door. My life is hopelessly crowded with all categories of junk; does no one else have this problem?

Oh, what the hell, maybe an octagonal mirror there, a

wind chime here is all it would take to turn this place around. I've already rearranged my entire life for my cats, what are a few small changes for the sake of ancient passed-down principals? Sure, the chi's flow in my house may be somewhat convoluted, but at least I know exactly where it will end up: The same corner of the bathroom where all the cat fur collects.

"How to" Guide for Managing
Your Human: A Warning

I thought I'd end this book on cats reflecting on another one I came across titled something like "Guide to Owning a Maine Coon Cat." At first this seemed like a reasonable-enough title, until it hit me the fallacy of being guided through such a thing, by a book or otherwise.

Sure, it's a good idea to set forth general knowledge about cats, but why does this one breed need a whole guide for itself? Was there something more to owning a Maine Coon cat that I didn't know about? I had to know, so I brought it home.

The book is filled with fascinating facts about the Maine Coon cat, the kind of thing that could provide hours of entertainment for a Maine Coon-cat-kook like me. I read on until I noticed that the authors were attributing a lot of characteristics to the breed, personality traits and ways of being in the world. That is where I started to feel, shall

I say?, uncomfortable. It is one thing to give advice about coping with cat dread-locks and proclivities for maladies, that sort of thing, it is altogether quite another to lay a big heavy head trip on Maine Coon cats about being born with this personality trait or that, as if they have no individuality and free will of their own.

The worst part is that I recently noticed that my own Maine Coon cat actually seems to have taken on some of these very personality attributes. The only thing I can think is that I must have left the book lying out. That, my friend, was a major mistake.

These types of "Guides" have no place in the home. Under no circumstances should you let your cat have access to one of these things. No animal should know so much about themselves besides humans, who are uniquely equipped for the weight of this knowledge thanks only to the most advanced sense of humor in the universe.

9

Cat Time Management for Life:
Fulfill Your Cat's Dreams Today!

In conclusion, always remember these *TMC* essentials:

-Cats really do need to work every little bit as much as we need them to.

-Chances are your cat's already working for you; your job is to figure out *how?*

-Never give up. There is no better way to spend *your* time than managing your cat's time.

-And never forget:

Right now is an *extremely exciting time to be a cat!*

Please be aware that every suggestion I've made is simply the most helpful advice I can offer at this time. You and your cat are free to chew on it, change it, or regurgitate it as I know you will.

In the end, perhaps the most wonderful thing I can tell you about managing your cat's time is this: You don't *have* to build your cat a home office or find him a new career to make him happy and achieve the kind of deep satisfaction that comes with something like success. Any decent use of time with your cat will eventually uncover the blueprint for bliss that already exists between you.

He's got the itch, and you know how to scratch. It's a match made in heaven.

>>><<<

About the Author's Cats

The cats behind *Time Management for Cats* are the same cats behind *Self Help for Cats*, the Wordpress blog. They are: Brody and Herman Panther, an inseparable duo of urban Oakland home kitties (see their pictures on the back cover). These savvy social networkers will soon be featured in their very own book about cat life in the modern cat hood titled *Cat Soup: Today's Special,* coming out really soon.

Brody and Herman's human and writer is humorist and library worker Alison F. Bowman. Alison's humor has been featured in the *Magazine of Fantasy and Science Fiction* and the *San Francisco Chronicle*, among others. Winner of the Best Soft Sci Fi Story of 2002, Alison's writing also received a certificate of excellence from the Cat Writers Association. *Time Management for Cats* is Alison and her cats' first published book.

Connect with Us Online at

AlisonBowman.com
SelfHelpforCats.net
and
TimeManagementforCats.com

>>><<<

If you enjoyed this book, please consider writing a review on your favorite book review site or at Smashwords.com. And tell a friend!
Thank you, for your time…

www.ingramcontent.com/pod-product-compliance
Lightning Source LLC
Chambersburg PA
CBHW070544030426
42337CB00016B/2342